CORNING®

W9-BVF-580

# HEARTY CHOICES FOR
# WINTER

# CONTENTS

Home COLLECTION MAISON

# French Onion Soup

Comfort food at its best on a cold winter evening, warming and satisfying!
**Makes 2 servings.**

| | | |
|---|---|---|
| 2 tbsp | *butter* | 30 mL |
| 2 cups | *thinly sliced onions* | 500 mL |
| ½ tsp | *sugar* | 2 mL |
| 2 | *cans (10oz/284 mL) beef consommé* | 2 |
| ¼ cup | *Madeira wine or sherry (optional)* | 50 mL |
| | *salt and pepper, to taste* | |
| 2 | *thick slices of French bread* | 2 |
| ½ cup | *shredded Swiss cheese* | 125 mL |

1. Melt butter over medium heat in a saucepan. Add onions and cook about 10 minutes, stirring occasionally. Add sugar and cook another 15 to 20 minutes over medium-low heat until onions are golden but not browned. Add consommé and Madeira (if using) and simmer 20 minutes.

2. Meanwhile, toast bread under the broiler for a few minutes until lightly browned on each side.

3. Add salt and pepper to soup. Pour soup into two ovenproof bowls. Put one piece of bread in each bowl on top of the soup and sprinkle cheese on the bread. Broil until cheese is melted and bubbly.

**CORNING RECOMMENDS**
CORNINGWARE® POP-INS™
16-oz Round FRENCH WHITE®
Casserole

# Roasted Garlic and Brie with Rosemary

This food is a wonderful, hearty combination of flavours perfect for a chill winter's eve.

**Makes 4 servings.**

| | | |
|---|---|---|
| 4 | *whole garlic bulbs* | 4 |
| ¼ cup | *olive oil* | 50 mL |
| ½ lb | *wedge of Brie* | 250 g |
| 1 tbsp | *crumbled dried rosemary* | 30 mL |
| | *sliced French bread or crackers* | |

1. Cut the top off each bulb of garlic so tops of cloves are visible. Put bulbs in a small baking dish. Drizzle with olive oil. Bake in a preheated 375°F (190°C) oven for 40 minutes or until golden brown and cloves begin to pop out of skins.
2. Remove garlic from baking dish and squeeze out individual cloves. Put cloves back into baking dish.
3. Set Brie on top of the garlic and put the dish back into the oven until the cheese has melted and spread over the garlic.
4. Remove from oven. Sprinkle with rosemary and serve hot with slices of French bread or crackers.

**CORNING RECOMMENDS**
CORNINGWARE® Little Dishes
15-oz FRENCH WHITE®
Oval Casserole with Lid

# Warm Cheese with Prosciutto

Melted cheese is a perennial favourite, whether it's dressed down as a grilled cheese sandwich or dressed up for company, like this.

**Makes 4–6 servings.**

| | | |
|---|---|---|
| 6 oz | goat cheese or feta | 175 g |
| 3 tbsp | pesto, homemade or store bought | 45 mL |
| 3 tbsp | olive oil | 45 mL |
| I tbsp | tomato paste | 15 mL |
| dash | Tabasco sauce or pepper flakes | dash |
| ½ tsp | freshly ground black pepper | 2 mL |
| ½ cup | prosciutto, diced | 125 mL |
| | green or black olives (optional) | |
| | French bread, toasted flat bread or pita chips | |

1. Slice or crumble cheese in a shallow ovenproof serving dish. Combine pesto, oil, tomato paste, Tabasco, pepper and prosciutto. Pour over cheese.
2. Heat cheese in a preheated 350°F (180°C) oven for 10 to 12 minutes, or until soft.
3. If using, arrange olives over cheese. Serve warm with bread or pita chips.

**CORNING RECOMMENDS**
CORNINGWARE® Little Dishes
15-oz FRENCH WHITE®
Oval Casserole

# Warm Portobello Mushroom Salad

An impressive salad that's often seen on restaurant menus. Now you know how quick and easy it is to prepare at home.

**Makes 4 servings.**

## Dressing

| | | |
|---|---|---|
| ⅓ cup | olive oil | 75 mL |
| ¼ cup | balsamic vinegar | 50 mL |
| 1 | garlic clove, minced | 1 |
| 2 tbsp | chopped fresh basil | 30 mL |
| 1 tbsp | Dijon mustard | 15 mL |
| | salt and pepper, to taste | |

## Salad

| | | |
|---|---|---|
| 2 tbsp | olive oil | 30 mL |
| 2 tbsp | balsamic vinegar | 30 mL |
| 2 | garlic cloves, minced | 2 |
| 4 | large Portobello mushrooms | 4 |
| 6 cups | mixed salad greens | 1.5 L |
| 2 | roasted red peppers, bottled or homemade | 2 |
| 1 | red onion, sliced | 1 |

1. Combine dressing ingredients in a small bowl and mix well.
2. To make salad, combine olive oil, vinegar and garlic. Remove stems from mushrooms then rinse the caps under cold water and pat dry. Pour marinade over mushroom caps and leave for 2 hours.
3. Sauté mushroom caps smooth side down in a skillet for about 5 minutes. Remove from heat.
4. Toss dressing with salad greens, then arrange greens on four salad plates. Place one sliced mushroom and half a sliced pepper on each plate, and top with slices of the red onion. Drizzle a little of the dressing over the mushrooms and peppers.

**CORNING RECOMMENDS**
PYREX® Originals™ 1-cup
Measuring Cup and
CORNINGWARE® Casual Elegance
White Flora™ 14" Embossed
Oval Platter

# Stuffed Mushrooms

Simple and scrumptious!

**Makes 4 servings.**

| | | |
|---|---|---|
| 20 | *large white mushrooms* | 20 |
| ½ cup | *feta cheese, crumbled* | 125 mL |
| ¼ tsp | *dried oregano* | 1 mL |
| 1 | *garlic clove, minced* | 1 |
| ½ cup | *black olives, pitted and chopped* | 125 mL |
| ¼ cup | *bread crumbs* | 50 mL |
| 2 tbsp | *olive oil* | 30 mL |

1. Preheat oven to 350°F (180°C).
2. Clean mushrooms and remove stems. Mix together cheese, oregano, garlic and olives and fill each mushroom.
3. Put mushrooms in a lightly greased 13 × 9-inch (3.5-L) baking dish. Drizzle olive oil over and bake for about 8 minutes.

## Cheese Stuffed Mushrooms

| | | |
|---|---|---|
| 20 | *large white mushrooms* | 20 |
| ¼ lb | *herbed soft cheese (such as Boursin)* | 125 g |

Fill the mushrooms with the cheese and bake as per directions given for the Stuffed Mushrooms.

# Ready-in-no-time Mushroom and Sausage Lasagna

What more can be said?

**Makes 8 servings.**

| | | |
|---|---|---|
| 2 tbsp | *olive oil* | 30 mL |
| 1 lb | *hot Italian sausage* | 500 g |
| 2 | *garlic cloves, crushed* | 2 |
| 1 lb | *mushrooms, sliced* | 500 g |
| 1 | *jar (28 oz / 796 mL) meatless spaghetti sauce* | 1 |
| 12 | *lasagna noodles* | 12 |
| 1 lb | *mozzarella cheese, shredded* | 500 g |
| 1 cup | *grated Parmesan cheese* | 250 mL |

<u>*Put One Away*</u>

Assemble lasagna in two casserole dishes. Bake one to serve 4 and freeze the other. To cook, thaw overnight in refrigerator and bake at 350°F (180°C) for 30 to 45 minutes. Let stand 15 minutes. Serve.

1. Heat 1 tbsp (15 mL) oil in a skillet over medium heat. Remove casings from sausages, crumble the meat into pieces and cook in oil until no longer pink. Remove sausage and drain fat. Add 1 tbsp (15 mL) oil to pan and sauté garlic and mushrooms for 5 minutes. Drain off any fat or juices and return sausage to pan along with spaghetti sauce. Reduce heat and simmer 10 minutes.

2. Meanwhile, cook noodles in a pot of boiling salted water until al dente, about 10 minutes. Drain and put them in a bowl of cold water until ready to use. Dry them on a clean kitchen towel when needed.

3. Heat oven to 350°F (180°C). Spread 1 cup (250 mL) sauce on the bottom of a large baking dish. Put a layer of 4 slightly overlapping noodles on top of the sauce. Cover the noodles with ⅓ of the remaining sauce, ⅓ of the mozzarella and ⅓ of the Parmesan. Cover with 4 more noodles, the sauce and cheeses then the remaining noodles, sauce and cheeses.

4. Bake for 30 to 45 minutes until browned and bubbly. Remove from oven and let stand 15 minutes before cutting.

# Sweet and Sour Pork Chops

These chops are juicy and tender and the sauce is delicious!
**Makes 4 servings.**

| | | |
|---|---|---|
| 1 tsp | *dry mustard* | 5 mL |
| 1 tsp | *garlic salt* | 5 mL |
| 1 tsp | *paprika* | 5 mL |
| 1 tsp | *salt* | 5 mL |
| ¼ tsp | *pepper* | 1 mL |
| ¼ cup | *flour* | 50 mL |
| 4 | *pork loin chops, centre cut* | 4 |
| 2 tbsp | *butter* | 30 mL |
| 1 cup | *apple juice* | 250 mL |
| 2 tbsp | *white vinegar* | 30 mL |
| 3 tbsp | *brown sugar* | 45 mL |
| 2 cups | *cooked white rice* | 500 mL |
| 3 | *green onions, chopped* | 3 |

1. Mix dry mustard, garlic salt, paprika, salt, pepper and flour together and put the mixture into a plastic bag.
2. Put pork chops, one at a time, into the bag and shake to coat the meat.
3. Melt butter in a 12-inch (30-cm) nonstick skillet and brown chops, turning them once.
4. Stir in apple juice, vinegar and sugar and simmer, uncovered, for 40 minutes until chops are no longer pink and the sauce has thickened.
5. Serve over rice and sprinkle with chopped green onions.

**CORNING RECOMMENDS**
PYREX® Originals™ 1-pt Measuring
Cup, REVERE® Nonstick 12" Skillet
and CORELLE® IMPRESSIONS®
Oceanview Dinner Plate

# Chicken Cacciatore

A comforting dish to dig into on a cold winter's night.

**Makes 4 servings.**

| | | |
|---|---|---|
| 4 | *single, boneless, skinless chicken breasts* | 4 |
| ½ cup | *flour* | 125 mL |
| ½ tsp | *salt* | 2 mL |
| ¼ tsp | *pepper* | 1 mL |
| 4 tbsp | *olive oil* | 60 mL |
| 2 | *garlic cloves, minced* | 2 |
| 1 | *large onion, sliced* | 1 |
| 4 cups | *mushrooms, sliced* | 1 L |
| 1 | *can (28 oz/796 mL) plum tomatoes* | 1 |
| ½ tsp | *sugar* | 2 mL |
| 1 ½ tsp | *dried basil* | 7 mL |
| 1 ½ tsp | *dried oregano* | 7 mL |

1. Cut chicken into 1-inch pieces. Put flour, salt and pepper into a plastic bag. Add chicken a few pieces at a time and toss to coat.
2. Heat 3 tbsp (45 mL) of olive oil in a 6-qt (6-L) stockpot and lightly brown chicken in batches.
3. Remove chicken. Add 1 tbsp (15 mL) oil to the pot and sauté garlic, onion and mushrooms over low heat until limp. Return chicken to pot.
4. Add tomatoes, sugar, basil and oregano. Bring to a boil, then simmer, covered, for 1 hour.
5. Serve over rice or pasta.

# Better-than-bottled Pasta Sauce

Delicious and very quick to make. You'll never want to open a bottle of spaghetti sauce again!

**Makes 4 servings.**

| | | |
|---|---|---|
| 2 | cans (28 oz / 796 mL) plum tomatoes | 2 |
| 4 tbsp | olive oil | 60 mL |
| 1 tsp | salt | 5 mL |
| 1 tsp | dried basil or oregano | 5 mL |
| 1 tsp | fennel seeds | 5 mL |
| ½ tsp | sugar | 2 mL |
| | generous grinding of black pepper | |
| 1 tsp | balsamic vinegar (optional) | 5 mL |

1. Drain almost all the juice from tomatoes. Process tomatoes briefly in a food processor.
2. Heat olive oil over medium-high heat in a 10-inch (25-cm) skillet. When oil is very hot, but not smoking, slowly pour in tomatoes. Reduce heat to medium.
3. Add salt, basil or oregano, fennel seeds, sugar, pepper and vinegar (if using). Stir well and adjust heat so mixture simmers. Do not cover.
4. For a very fresh taste, simmer for 10 minutes; for a thicker sauce, simmer for up to 30 minutes. Serve over pasta with grated Parmesan cheese.

## Some Like It Hot

| | | |
|---|---|---|
| | Better-than-bottled Pasta Sauce recipe, above | |
| 1 tsp | crushed red chili peppers | 5 mL |
| 5 | garlic cloves (pressed, minced or cut into chunks) | 5 |

Add the crushed red peppers and garlic when adding the other seasonings. Cook as directed.

**CORNING RECOMMENDS**
REVERE® Copper Clad Bottom
10" Skillet and CORELLE®
IMPRESSIONS® Sand Art
1-qt Serving Bowl

# Chicken Con Queso

This is a great way to use leftover chicken or turkey. If leftovers aren't available, poach or bake some boneless chicken breasts and use those instead.
**Makes 4 servings.**

| | | |
|---|---|---|
| ¼ cup | *butter* | 50 mL |
| 1 | *large onion, chopped* | 1 |
| 2 | *garlic cloves, minced* | 2 |
| ⅓ cup | *flour* | 75 mL |
| 1 ½ cups | *chicken stock, hot* | 375 mL |
| 1 ½ cups | *milk, hot* | 375 mL |
| 3 cups | *grated cheddar cheese* | 750 mL |
| ¼ cup | *chopped fresh parsley* | 50 mL |
| ¼ cup | *chopped fresh coriander* | 50 mL |
| 2 tbsp | *tomato paste* | 30 mL |
| 1 tsp | *chili powder* | 5 mL |
| ½ tsp | *dried oregano* | 2 mL |
| ¼ cup | *diced green chilies, drained* | 50 mL |
| 3 | *green onions, chopped* | 3 |
| | *salt and pepper to taste* | |
| 3 cups | *diced cooked chicken or turkey* | 750 mL |
| 1 cup | *corn chips, crumbled* | 250 mL |

1. Melt butter in a large saucepan. Cook onion and garlic until soft. Add flour and cook over medium heat for 4 minutes. Whisk in stock and milk and cook, stirring often, until sauce thickens, about 8 minutes.
2. Remove from heat and stir in 2 cups (500 mL) cheese, parsley, coriander, tomato paste, chili powder, oregano, chilies and onions. Season with salt and pepper. Stir in chicken.
3. Pour mixture into a casserole dish. Sprinkle with remaining cheese and chips. Bake at 350°F (180°C) for 25 minutes, or until heated through. Serve with rice.

*Put One Away*

Prepare this recipe up to step 3. Pour into two smaller casseroles; complete one as per the directions and freeze the other for later use. Thaw frozen casserole, add ½ cup (125 mL) grated cheddar and ½ cup (125 mL) corn chips and bake as instructed.

**CORNING RECOMMENDS**
CORNINGWARE® FRENCH WHITE® 2 ½-qt Oval Casserole with Cradle and CORELLE® IMPRESSIONS® Enhancements Dinner Plate

# Southwestern Chicken

This will warm your bones and it's so easy you can prepare it for the family to enjoy at the end of a busy day.

**Makes 6 servings.**

| | | |
|---|---|---|
| 1 tbsp | olive oil | 15 mL |
| 1 | onion, finely diced | 1 |
| 3 | garlic cloves, minced | 3 |
| 1 | can (28 oz/796 mL) plum tomatoes, puréed | 1 |
| ¼ cup | honey | 50 mL |
| 2 tbsp | lime juice or red wine vinegar | 30 mL |
| ½ tsp | cinnamon | 2 mL |
| ½ tsp | chili powder | 2 mL |
| ¼ tsp | red pepper flakes | 1 mL |
| ½ tsp | salt | 2 mL |
| | pepper, to taste | |
| 1 | tin (14 oz/398 mL) mild green chilies, rinsed | 1 |
| 1 tsp | vegetable or olive oil | 5 mL |
| 6 | single, boneless, skinless chicken breasts | 6 |
| | lime wedges or cucumber slices, for garnish | |

1. Heat oil in a medium saucepan over medium-high heat. Add onions and garlic. Cook 5 minutes until softened. Add puréed tomatoes and cook 15 minutes over medium heat until sauce is thick.

2. Add honey, lime juice, cinnamon, chili powder, pepper flakes, salt, pepper and chilies. Simmer 5 to 8 minutes. Reserve. Adjust seasonings.

3. Brush nonstick skillet or grill pan with oil. Heat to medium-high. Brown chicken breasts 2 to 3 minutes per side until golden brown. Place in a single layer in a baking dish. Pour sauce over top.

4. Bake chicken at 350°F (180°C) for 20 to 25 minutes, or until chicken is no longer pink inside. Serve garnished with lime wedges or cucumber slices.

**CORNING RECOMMENDS**

VISIONS® Cranberry 4-qt Large Oval Roaster with Cover

# Oven-barbecued Garlicky Chicken Wings

These wings are so delicious, you'll want to find the little bit of time it takes to make wings "from scratch" at home.

**Makes 4–6 servings.**

| | | |
|---|---|---|
| 4 lbs | *wings, trimmed and separated* | 2 kg |
| I cup | *ketchup* | 250 mL |
| ⅔ cup | *white vinegar* | 150 mL |
| ⅔ cup | *water* | 150 mL |
| I tbsp | *sugar* | 15 mL |
| 2 tbsp | *Dijon mustard* | 30 mL |
| 2 tbsp | *butter* | 30 mL |
| 2 tsp | *salt* | 10 mL |
| 3 tbsp | *Worcestershire sauce* | 45 mL |
| I tbsp | *hot sauce or 1 tsp (5 mL) Tabasco sauce* | 15 mL |
| 6 | *garlic cloves, minced* | 6 |

1. Heat oven to 400°F (200°C). Place chicken wings in a single layer in a large baking dish. Bake chicken while making sauce.
2. To make sauce, place remaining ingredients in saucepan. Bring to a boil, reduce heat and simmer 20 minutes.
3. Pour half of the sauce over wings, and bake 20 minutes. Pour rest of sauce over, and bake another 20 minutes. Serve.

**CORNING RECOMMENDS**
CORNINGWARE® Casual
Elegance White Flora™ 2 1/4-qt
Rectangular Dish with Cover

# Hot Black Bean Chili

This makes a delicious change from the red kidney bean variety but — eater beware! — it's hot, hot, hot!

**Makes 4 servings.**

### *Avocado Salsa*

| | | |
|---|---|---|
| I | ripe avocado, very finely diced | I |
| ½ | red onion, finely chopped | ½ |
| 2 tbsp | coriander, chopped | 30 mL |
| I | lime, juiced | I |
| 4 drops | Tabasco sauce | 4 drops |
| 2 tbsp | salsa, homemade or storebought | 30 mL |

| | | |
|---|---|---|
| 2 tbsp | olive oil | 30 mL |
| 2 | large onions, chopped in large dice | 2 |
| 4 | garlic cloves, crushed | 4 |
| I lb | round or sirloin beef steak, finely diced | 500 g |
| I tbsp | flour | 15 mL |
| I | can (28 oz / 796 mL) plum tomatoes, chopped, with juice | I |
| I | can (19 oz / 540 mL) black beans, drained | I |
| ½ cup | fresh chopped coriander leaves and stems | 125 mL |
| 4 tbsp | pickled jalapeños, drained | 60 mL |
| I | red pepper, chopped | I |
| I | lime | I |
| | salt, to taste | |
| 4 tbsp | yogurt or sour cream | 60 mL |

### *Put One Away*

Double the recipe, put half in casserole and freeze. Thaw in refrigerator, then bake at 350°F (180°C) for 30 to 40 minutes, or until heated through.

**CORNING RECOMMENDS**
REVERE® Copper Clad Bottom 6-qt Stockpot and CORELLE® IMPRESSIONS® Callaway Salad/Pasta Bowl

1. Heat olive oil in 6-qt (6-L) stockpot, add onions and sauté until clear. Add garlic and sauté another minute. Remove vegetables from pot with slotted spoon, leaving as much oil as possible in pan.
2. Add beef to pan and brown. Stir in flour to coat browned beef. Add onions, garlic, tomatoes, beans and coriander. Bring to a boil, then reduce heat. Cover and simmer for I hour.
3. Add jalapeños, red pepper, juice from lime and salt to taste. Simmer for another 30 minutes.
4. To make Avocado Salsa, combine all ingredients.
5. Serve chili on its own, with yogurt or sour cream, and Avocado Salsa, or over rice.

# Lemon-glazed Turkey Cutlets

Turkey makes a nice change from chicken, and this is a great dish because you don't have to buy or prepare the full turkey to roast.

**Makes 4 servings.**

| | | |
|---|---|---|
| 1 ½ lb | *single turkey breast, boned and skinned* | 750 g |
| 2 tbsp | *vegetable oil* | 30 mL |
| 2 tbsp | *lemon juice* | 30 mL |
| 2 tsp | *Dijon mustard* | 10 mL |
| ½ tsp | *dried oregano* | 2 mL |
| ½ tsp | *dried rosemary* | 2 mL |
| 3 | *garlic cloves, minced* | 3 |
| ½ tsp | *salt* | 2 mL |
| | *freshly ground pepper* | |
| 1 tsp | *vegetable oil* | 5 mL |
| 1 tsp | *butter* | 5 mL |
| ¼ cup | *lemon juice* | 75 mL |
| ½ cup | *chicken stock, homemade or canned* | 125 mL |

1. Cut turkey breast on the diagonal into thick cutlets.
2. Combine oil, lemon juice, mustard, oregano, rosemary, garlic, salt and pepper and rub into turkey. Marinate several hours in refrigerator.
3. Heat vegetable oil and butter in a nonstick pan. Cook turkey cutlets in batches until brown on each side, about 5 minutes per side. Place browned turkey in ovenproof pan. Finish cooking in 350°F (180°C) oven, about 10 to 12 minutes. Time will depend on thickness of cutlets. Do not overcook. Remove turkey cutlets to serving dish or plates and keep warm.
4. Place cooking pan on heat, at medium-high setting, and deglaze with lemon juice and chicken stock. Reduce juices and pour over turkey before serving.

# Baked Pork Chops with
## Savoy Cabbage

Savoy cabbage is the pretty cabbage with curly leaves. Try it for a nice change.
**Makes 6 servings.**

| | | |
|---|---|---|
| 2 tbsp | *olive oil* | 30 mL |
| 1 | *onion, sliced* | 1 |
| 2 | *garlic cloves, minced* | 2 |
| 6 cups | *shredded Savoy or green cabbage* | 1.5 L |
| 1 tsp | *chopped fresh thyme (¼ tsp / 1 mL dried)* | 5 mL |
| | *salt and pepper* | |
| 6 | *pork chops, fat trimmed* | 6 |
| ½ cup | *chicken stock or white wine* | 125 mL |
| ½ cup | *whipping cream* | 125 mL |
| 1 cup | *bread crumbs* | 250 mL |
| ½ cup | *grated cheddar cheese* | 125 mL |
| ¼ cup | *chopped parsley* | 50 mL |

1. Heat 1 tbsp (15 mL) olive oil in a large skillet over medium-high heat. Add onion. Cook 2 minutes until softened. Add garlic and cook 1 minute. Stir in cabbage. Stir and cook 5 to 6 minutes until cooked. Season with thyme, salt and pepper. Place half of cabbage in lightly oiled 8-cup (2-L) baking dish. Reserve rest of cabbage.

2. Heat remaining oil in pan. Pat pork chops dry. Put in skillet and cook on both sides until golden brown. Place over cabbage in baking dish. Season with salt and pepper. Spoon remaining cabbage over pork chops.

3. Add chicken stock and cream to skillet. Stir well over medium-high heat to release any bits in pan. Pour over cabbage.

4. Combine bread crumbs, cheese and parsley. Sprinkle over cabbage.

5. Bake in preheated 350°F (180°C) oven for 30 minutes. Serve.

# Corn Chowder with Bacon

When it's cold outside, there's nothing like a big bowl of steaming soup!
**Makes 4–6 servings.**

| | | |
|---|---|---|
| ½ cup | butter | 125 mL |
| 2 | onions, finely chopped | 2 |
| 2 | garlic cloves, minced | 2 |
| 2 | celery ribs, chopped | 2 |
| ¼ cup | all-purpose flour | 50 mL |
| 2 cups | milk | 500 mL |
| 3 cups | chicken stock | 750 mL |
| 3 | medium potatoes, peeled and diced | 3 |
| 1 tsp | dried thyme | 5 mL |
| 1 ½ cups | corn niblets | 375 mL |
| ½ cup | heavy cream (optional) | 125 mL |
| | salt and pepper, to taste | |

*Optional garnishes: slices of bacon, cooked crisp and chopped, chopped green onions and chopped parsley*

1. Melt butter in a 2-qt (2-L) saucepan. Add onions, garlic and celery. Cook until fragrant but do not brown. Add flour. Cook over medium heat, stirring, for 5 minutes. Cool slightly.
2. Whisk in milk and chicken stock. Bring to a boil. Add potatoes and thyme. Reduce heat, cover and cook until potatoes are tender, about 20 minutes.
3. Add corn and cream, if using, and cook another 5 to 8 minutes. Season with salt and pepper.
4. Serve garnished with bacon bits, onions and parsley.

**CORNING RECOMMENDS**
PYREX® Originals™ 1-pt Measuring Cup, REVERE® Copper Clad Bottom 2-qt Saucepan with CORNINGWARE® 15-oz GRAB -IT® Bowl with White Plastic Cover

# Vegetable and Smoked Salmon Hash

This dish is just as delicious if the smoked salmon is replaced with another smoked fish or cooked sausage, smoked chicken or leftover turkey.

**Makes 4 servings.**

| | | |
|---|---|---|
| 2 tbsp | *olive oil* | 30 mL |
| I | *large onion, thinly sliced* | I |
| 2 | *garlic cloves, minced* | 2 |
| I | *red pepper, peeled and thinly sliced* | I |
| I | *small zucchini, cut in 2-inch (5-cm) julienne strips* | I |
| 2 tbsp | *butter or olive oil (or more)* | 30 mL |
| 3–4 cups | *julienned cooked potatoes (with skin on)* | 750 mL–I L |
| 6–8 oz | *smoked salmon, diced* | 175–250 g |
| 2 tbsp | *chopped fresh dill* | 30 mL |
| 2 tbsp | *parsley* | 30 mL |
| | *salt and pepper* | |
| 4 | *fried or poached eggs (optional)* | 4 |

1. Heat oil in a large nonstick skillet. Add onion, garlic and pepper and cook over medium heat until very soft, at least 10 minutes. Add zucchini halfway through.
2. Increase heat and add remaining butter or oil and potatoes. Cook until potatoes are heated through and starting to brown. When potatoes are warm, add salmon, herbs and salt and pepper.
3. Serve on heated plates with eggs, if desired.

# Bistro Ragout with Wild Mushrooms

Wild mushrooms in a beef stew add a whole new dimension of taste!
**Makes 4–6 servings.**

| | | |
|---|---|---|
| ½ oz | dried Porcini mushrooms | 50 g |
| 1 cup | warm water | 250 mL |
| 2 tbsp | vegetable oil | 30 mL |
| 2 lb | cubed lean stewing beef | 1 kg |
| 2 tbsp | flour | 30 mL |
| 3 | onions, sliced | 3 |
| 4 | garlic cloves, minced | 4 |
| 3 cups | beef stock, canned or homemade | 750 mL |
| 2 tbsp | tomato paste | 30 mL |
| 2 tsp | Worcestershire sauce | 10 mL |
| 1 tsp | salt | 5 mL |
| ½ tsp | freshly ground pepper | 2 mL |
| ½ tsp | dried tarragon | 2 mL |
| 1 lb | potatoes, cubed | 500 g |
| 2 tbsp | chopped parsley | 30 mL |

1. Rinse mushrooms if they are sandy. Pour water over dried mushrooms and let soften 20 minutes. Strain and reserve liquid. Chop mushrooms and reserve. Strain soaking liquid through cheesecloth or clean dish towel.

2. Heat oil in large saucepan over medium-high heat. Dust beef with flour. Brown well on all sides, adding more oil if necessary. Do not crowd pan. Cook in batches if necessary. Remove beef. Reserve.

3. Add onions and garlic to pan along with ¼ cup (50 mL) stock. Scrape bits from pan bottom. Cook onions and garlic 6 minutes or until soft. Add remaining stock, tomato paste, Worcestershire sauce, salt, pepper, tarragon, reserved mushroom liquid, mushrooms and meat. Bring to a boil. Reduce heat. Cover and simmer 1 ½ to 2 hours until meat is tender. Stir occasionally to prevent sticking.

4. Add potatoes and cook 15 to 20 minutes until tender. Stir in parsley. Serve.

# Chunky Vegetable and Split Pea Soup

A hearty soup rich with flavour and thick enough to make a meal.
**Makes 8 servings.**

| | | |
|---|---|---|
| 2 tbsp | *olive oil* | 30 mL |
| 2 | *onions, diced* | 2 |
| 2 | *garlic cloves, minced* | 2 |
| 3 | *celery ribs, coarsely chopped* | 3 |
| 2 | *carrots, coarsely chopped* | 2 |
| ½ cup | *yellow split peas* | 125 mL |
| ½ cup | *green split peas* | 125 mL |
| 8 cups | *chicken or vegetable stock* | 2 L |
| ½ tsp | *dried rosemary, crumbled* | 2 mL |
| ½ tsp | *dried thyme* | 2 mL |
| 1 | *bay leaf* | 1 |
| 2 | *parsnips, peeled, cut in medium dice* | 2 |
| 2 | *sweet potatoes, peeled, cut in medium dice* | 2 |
| ½ cup | *pasta, such as macaroni or penne* | 125 mL |
| 2 cups | *chopped cabbage* | 500 mL |
| | *salt and pepper, to taste* | |
| ⅓ cup | *chopped parsley, for garnish* | 75 mL |
| | *grated Parmesan cheese and diced kielbasa or ham, for garnish* | |

1. Heat oil in a large Dutch oven. Cook onions and garlic until soft and fragrant. Stir in celery and carrots. Cook 3 minutes. Add peas, stock and herbs. Bring to a boil. Reduce heat. Cover and simmer over medium-low heat for 50 minutes or until peas are just tender.

2. Add parsnips, potatoes and pasta. Return to a boil. Cover and cook 15 to 20 minutes, adding cabbage during last 5 minutes of cooking.

3. Remove bay leaf. Season soup with salt and pepper to taste. Stir in parsley just before serving. Garnish each serving of soup with cheese or diced meat.

# Roast Pork Loin with Mushrooms

A delicious collection of robust flavours for a fancy dinner when the weather turns cold. Roasted potatoes and carrots will round out the meal nicely.

**Makes 6 servings.**

| | | |
|---|---|---|
| 1 tsp | salt | 5 mL |
| | freshly ground pepper, to taste | |
| 1 tbsp | Dijon mustard | 15 mL |
| 3 tbsp | chopped fresh rosemary or 2 tsp (10 mL) dried | 45 mL |
| 3 | garlic cloves, minced | 3 |
| 3 lb | pork loin roast, trimmed and tied | 1.5 kg |
| 2 tbsp | olive oil | 30 mL |
| 2 | medium onions, sliced | 2 |
| ½ lb | mushrooms, quartered | 250 g |
| 2 tbsp | tomato sauce | 30 mL |
| 1 cup | white wine | 250 mL |
| 2 ½ cups | stock (chicken or veal), homemade or store bought | 625 mL |
| 1 tbsp | cornstarch | 15 mL |
| | rosemary or parsley sprigs, for garnish | |

1. In a small bowl, make a paste of salt, pepper, mustard, half the rosemary and 1 clove minced garlic. Rub over pork.

2. Heat oil in a skillet and brown meat on all sides. Transfer to a roasting pan.

3. Cook remaining garlic and onions in skillet until softened, about 4 minutes. Add mushrooms and cook until softened, another 4 minutes. Add remaining rosemary, tomato sauce and white wine. Reduce sauce over high heat until syrupy. Add stock and pour mixture around roast. Cover and roast in a preheated 325°F (160°C) oven for 1 hour. Remove cover, increase heat to 425°F (225°C) and continue to cook 25 minutes or until juices run clear. Remove roast and keep warm.

4. Place sauce over high heat and reduce 5 minutes. Combine cornstarch with 1 tbsp (15 mL) water and stir into sauce. Cook 1 to 2 minutes. Season to taste. Carve roast, add garnish, and serve with sauce.

# Macaroni and Cheese

If this dish was called "Pasta and Creamy Cheese Sauce", it would probably command a lot more respect! Respect or no, this baked macaroni and cheese should be in the repertoire of every family because it's just so plain good.

**Makes 4 servings.**

| ½ lb | macaroni or other small pasta | 500 g |
|---|---|---|
| 1 ½ cup | milk | 375 mL |
| ½ cup | cream (table, half-and-half or whipping cream) | 125 mL |
| 2 tbsp | butter | 30 mL |
| 3 tbsp | flour | 45 mL |
| | salt and pepper, to taste | |
| 2 cups | grated cheddar cheese | 500 mL |

## Put One Away

Double the recipe. Pour half in a buttered casserole dish, cover well and freeze. Thaw in refrigerator and bake for 40 to 45 minutes at 350°F (180°C).

**CORNING RECOMMENDS**

CORNINGWARE® Classics™ Blue Velvet 2-qt Covered Casserole with Sculptured PYREX® 3-cup Serving Bowl

1. Preheat oven to 350°F (180°C). Bring large pot of water to a boil. Add macaroni and cook until barely tender, about 6 minutes. Drain.
2. Heat milk and cream in microwave until hot.
3. Melt butter in large saucepan, stir in flour and cook for 2 minutes. Slowly add hot milk and cream, then salt and pepper and cook over medium heat until thickened. Stir in cheese.
4. When cheese has melted, add macaroni and stir well to blend.
5. Butter a casserole dish. Spoon macaroni and cheese mixture into it and bake for 25 to 30 minutes, or until hot and bubbly.

# Roasted Potatoes Everybody Loves

Make more of these than you think you'll need; everybody loves these crunchy roasted potatoes.

**Makes 6 servings.**

| | | |
|---|---|---|
| ¼ cup | *olive oil* | 50 mL |
| 1 tbsp | *vegetable oil* | 15 mL |
| 4 lbs | *potatoes* | 2 kg |
| 1 tsp | *salt* | 5 mL |
| | *salt, to taste* | |

1. Preheat oven to 425°F (225°C). Pour oils into 9-qt (9-L) open roasting pan or baking dish, and place pan in upper half of oven.

2. Peel the potatoes and cut into rough chunks. Put in 3-qt (3-L) saucepan, cover with water, add 1 tsp (5 mL) salt and cover. Bring to boil, reduce heat and simmer for 10 minutes, or until the outside of the potato pieces can be easily pierced with a knife. Do not completely cook potatoes.

3. Drain water off potatoes, replace lid on saucepan and vigorously shake pan. Potatoes should appear roughed up.

4. Remove open roasting pan from oven and carefully tip potato pieces into pan. Use a long-handled spoon or spatula to toss potatoes with oil. Each piece should be lightly coated.

5. Spread potatoes evenly over pan in a single layer and sprinkle generously with salt.

6. Return pan to oven and bake for 45 to 50 minutes or until evenly browned. Serve.

## *Roasted Sweet Potatoes*

Follow the recipe above, substituting sweet potatoes for the white potatoes. Sprinkle with dried rosemary during baking.

**CORNING RECOMMENDS**
CORNINGWARE® Classics™ Blue
Velvet 4-qt Open Roaster

# Cheese-topped Green Beans with Bacon

When green beans are springing from your garden, you'll want to eat them with a little butter. But when they get a bit tired, in winter, the combination of green beans, bacon and cheese is a complete winner.

**Makes 6 servings.**

| | | |
|---|---|---|
| I lb | *green beans* | 500 g |
| 6 | *slices bacon, finely diced* | 6 |
| ½ cup | *finely diced onion* | 125 mL |
| ¼ cup | *flour* | 50 mL |
| I ½ cup | *chicken stock (homemade or canned)* | 375 mL |
| | *pepper, to taste* | |
| I cup | *Swiss cheese, grated* | 250 mL |
| 2 tbsp | *Parmesan cheese, grated* | 30 mL |

1. Bring water to boil in 2-qt (2-L) saucepan. Add beans and cook for 3 to 5 minutes until beans are beginning to soften. Drain and set aside.
2. Preheat oven to 350°F (180°C).
3. In skillet, cook bacon with onion over medium heat until bacon is browned and onions are soft. Stir in flour, then gradually add stock and pepper and cook until sauce is thickened.
4. Stir green beans into sauce and pour mixture into well-greased 2-qt (2-L) casserole dish. Sprinkle cheeses over top and bake for 30 minutes.

# Wild Rice Waldorf Salad

Once upon a time Waldorf Salad meant apples and mayonnaise. We've come a long way in how we interpret food.

**Makes 8 servings.**

| | | |
|---|---|---|
| 1 cup | *wild rice* | 250 mL |
| 1 cup | *diced celery* | 250 mL |
| 2 | *red apples, diced* | 2 |
| ½ cup | *golden raisins* | 125 mL |
| ½ cup | *dried cranberries* | 125 mL |
| ½ cup | *toasted\* sunflower seeds or walnut pieces* | 125 mL |
| ¼ cup | *chopped mint* | 50 mL |
| ¼ cup | *chopped parsley* | 50 mL |
| ⅓ cup | *mayonnaise* | 75 mL |
| ¼ cup | *lemon juice* | 50 mL |
| 2 tbsp | *orange juice concentrate or apple juice* | 30 mL |
| 1 tsp | *salt* | 5 mL |
| ¼ tsp | *black pepper* | 1 mL |
| 6–8 | *lettuce leaves* | 6–8 |

* Toast sunflower seeds or walnuts in 350°F (180°C) oven for 6 to 8 minutes, or until starting to colour.

1. Put rice in a medium saucepan. Add water to cover by 2 inches (5 cm). Bring to a boil and cook uncovered for 45 minutes, or until just tender. Add extra water if necessary during cooking. Drain rice and rinse with cold water to cool.

2. Place rice in a large mixing bowl. Add celery, apples, raisins, cranberries, sunflower seeds, mint and parsley. Toss to combine.

3. In a small bowl, whisk together mayonnaise, lemon juice, orange juice concentrate, salt and pepper. Add to rice and mix thoroughly. If time permits, refrigerate for 1 to 2 hours to blend flavours.

4. To serve, arrange in serving bowl lined with lettuce leaves.

# Potato and Turnip Gratin

A gratin is a fancy way of serving plain vegetables. Turnip never tasted this good before!

**Makes 6 servings.**

| | | |
|---|---|---|
| 1 lb | *turnip (rutabaga), cut into cubes* | 500 g |
| 1 ½ lb | *potatoes, cut into cubes* | 750 g |
| 2 | *medium onions, thinly sliced* | 2 |
| 1 cup | *sour cream* | 250 mL |
| 1 ½ tbsp | *flour* | 20 mL |
| 2 tbsp | *butter, melted* | 30 mL |
| ½ tsp | *salt* | 2 mL |
| | *pepper, to taste* | |
| ½ cup | *grated Parmesan cheese, plus 2 tbsp (30 mL)* | 125 mL |

1. Cook turnip in boiling water for 15 minutes. Add potatoes and onions and cook another 5 minutes. Drain, reserving ½ cup (125 mL) cooking liquid.
2. Whisk together sour cream, reserved cooking liquid, flour, butter, salt and pepper. Toss together with vegetables and ½ cup (125 mL) Parmesan.
3. Spoon into greased shallow casserole dish. Sprinkle with remaining Parmesan. Bake at 350°F (180°C) for 1 to 1 ½ hours or until vegetables are tender. Cool slightly before serving.

# Baked Maple-glazed Carrots

Maple and carrots are a natural combination. The sweetness of this dish should have even reluctant vegetable-eaters asking for more!

**Makes 4 servings.**

| | | |
|---|---|---|
| 2 tbsp | *butter* | 30 mL |
| 2 tbsp | *brown sugar* | 30 mL |
| 2 tbsp | *maple syrup* | 30 mL |
| 1 lb | *carrots* | 500 g |

1. Preheat oven to 350°F (180°C).
2. Combine butter, sugar and maple syrup.
3. Peel carrots and cut into narrow lengthwise strips. Toss with butter mixture. Bake for 35 minutes, or until carrots are tender and sauce has thickened.

## *Sweet Basil Carrots*

**Makes 4 servings.**

| | | |
|---|---|---|
| 1 lb | *carrots, sliced* | 500 g |
| 1 tbsp | *butter* | 15 mL |
| 1 tbsp | *sugar* | 15 mL |
| ½ tsp | *dried basil* | 2 mL |

Put carrots in a saucepan of boiling water over medium heat. Cook for about 10 minutes, or until carrots are tender crisp. Drain and add butter, sugar and basil to the carrots and toss until butter has melted.

# Dried Fruit Compote

This compote can be served warm or cold for breakfast or brunch. For a dessert, serve with pound cake, angel cake, crêpes or ice cream.

**Makes 8 servings.**

| | | |
|---|---|---|
| 2 cups | *dry white wine* | 500 mL |
| 2 cups | *orange or apricot juice* | 500 mL |
| ¼ cup | *honey* | 50 mL |
| | *zest from 1 lemon* | |
| 2 tbsp | *lemon juice* | 30 mL |
| I | *cinnamon stick* | I |
| 6 | *whole cloves* | 6 |
| I ½ cups | *dried apricots, halved* | 375 mL |
| I ½ cups | *prunes, halved* | 375 mL |
| I ½ cups | *dried apples or pears, cut in strips* | 375 mL |
| ½ cup | *dried cherries (if available)* | 125 mL |

1. In a medium saucepan, combine wine, orange juice, honey, lemon zest, lemon juice, cinnamon stick and cloves. Bring to a boil.
2. Add dried fruit. Return to a boil.
3. Cover, reduce heat and simmer 15 minutes until fruit is tender but not soft.

**CORNING RECOMMENDS**
Sculptured PYREX® 4½-qt Salad
Bowl with Plastic Storage Cover

# Baked Apples

The aroma of apples baking on a frosty night is welcoming, but the taste is so good, don't wait until winter to make this easy dessert.

**Makes 4 servings.**

| | | |
|---|---|---|
| 4 | *large apples* | 4 |
| 2 tbsp | *brown sugar* | 30 mL |
| 2 tbsp | *raisins or dried cranberries* | 30 mL |
| 2 tbsp | *granola* | 30 mL |
| ½ tsp | *cinnamon* | 2 mL |
| 2 tsp | *butter* | 10 mL |
| ½ cup | *apple juice* | 125 mL |

1. Preheat oven to 375°F (190°C).
2. Remove the core of each apple being careful not to go through the bottom. Pare a ½-inch (1.2-cm) band of skin from around the top of each apple. Put the apples in a baking dish.
3. Mix sugar, raisins or cranberries and granola and cinnamon together and fill the apples with this mixture. Dot the top of each apple with butter and add the juice to the dish. Bake until the apples are tender, 40 to 90 minutes, depending on the type of apple. Remove from the oven. Baste apples with juices and serve.

**CORNING RECOMMENDS**
CORNINGWARE® Classics™
Fruit Basket 2-qt Covered Casserole
and CORELLE® IMPRESSIONS®
Enhancements Soup/Cereal Bowl

# Peach Crumb Pie

You can replace some of the peaches with fresh or frozen raspberries or with rhubarb. If using rhubarb, increase sugar to ¾ cup (175 mL).

**Makes 6 servings.**

| | | |
|---|---|---|
| 1 ½ cups | *all-purpose flour* | 375 mL |
| 1 tbsp | *sugar* | 15 mL |
| ½ tsp | *salt* | 2 mL |
| ⅓ cup | *cold butter, cut into small pieces* | 75 mL |
| ⅓ cup | *cold lard or shortening, cut into small pieces* | 75 mL |
| ¼ cup | *cold water (or more)* | 50 mL |
| 6 cups | *peach slices* | 1.5 L |
| ½ cup | *sugar* | 125 mL |
| 2 tsp | *lemon juice* | 10 mL |
| 3 tbsp | *instant tapioca* | 45 mL |
| ½ tsp | *ground cinnamon* | 2 mL |
| 2 tsp | *grated lemon rind* | 10 mL |
| ⅓ cup | *brown sugar* | 75 mL |
| ⅓ cup | *all-purpose flour* | 75 mL |
| ¼ cup | *cold butter, cut into bits* | 50 mL |

1. To prepare pastry, combine flour, sugar and salt in a large bowl. Cut in butter and lard until they are in tiny bits. Add water and combine to form a dough. Wrap and refrigerate for 20 minutes. Roll dough out to fit a deep 9-inch (23-cm) pie pan. Form a high edge and crimp it.
2. To prepare filling, combine peach slices with sugar and lemon juice and let stand 10 minutes, then stir in tapioca and cinnamon. Pour filling into prepared crust.
3. Bake at 425°F (225°C) for 20 minutes. Reduce heat to 350°F (180°C) and bake for 30 minutes. Combine lemon rind, brown sugar, flour and butter and spread over peaches. Bake another 10 to 15 minutes or until topping is golden. Cool pie completely before serving.

# Butterscotch Pudding

Enjoy this old-fashioned favourite again and don't forget the big dollop of freshly whipped cream on top!

**Makes 4 servings.**

| | | |
|---|---|---|
| ¼ cup | *unsalted butter* | 50 mL |
| 1 cup | *dark brown sugar* | 250 mL |
| 3 | *egg yolks* | 3 |
| 3 tbsp | *cornstarch* | 45 mL |
| | *pinch of salt* | |
| 2 ½ cups | *milk* | 625 mL |
| 2 tbsp | *unsalted butter* | 30 mL |
| 1 tsp | *vanilla* | 5 mL |
| ½ tsp | *cider vinegar* | 2 mL |
| | *whipped cream and strawberries, for garnish* | |

1. Melt butter in a heavy saucepan. Add sugar and cook 3 minutes until bubbling. Remove from heat.
2. In a mixing bowl, combine egg yolks, cornstarch, salt and ½ cup (125 mL) milk. Mix well until cornstarch is dissolved. Stir in remaining milk. (If saucepan is not heavy, combine milk and sugar mixture in top part of double boiler.) Pour milk mixture into sugar. Cook over medium heat, stirring constantly until mixture thickens.
3. Remove from heat and stir in butter and vanilla. When butter is incorporated, stir in vinegar.
4. Pour into individual serving dishes. Cool. Garnish with freshly whipped cream and a fanned strawberry.

# Chocolate Marble Cheesecake

What a luscious winter dessert when only chocolate seems to fit the bill!
**Makes 10-12 servings.**

| | | |
|---|---|---|
| 1 ½ cups | *chocolate wafer crumbs* | 375 mL |
| 4 tbsp | *melted butter* | 60 mL |
| 2 tbsp | *sugar* | 30 mL |
| 3 | *packages (8 oz/750 g) cream cheese* | 3 |
| 1 cup | *sugar* | 250 mL |
| 3 tbsp | *flour* | 45 mL |
| 2 tbsp | *Amaretto liqueur* | 30 mL |
| ½ tsp | *vanilla* | 2 mL |
| 3 | *eggs* | 3 |
| 4 oz | *semi-sweet chocolate, melted* | 112 g |
| 2 oz | *semi-sweet chocolate, in squares, for garnish* | 60 g |

1. Preheat oven to 325°F (160°C).
2. To make crust, combine crumbs, butter and sugar. Press mixture into bottom of a 9-inch (23-cm) springform pan. Bake for 10 minutes. Remove from oven. Increase oven temperature to 425°F (225°C).
3. To make filling, in a large mixing bowl, beat cream cheese, sugar, flour, Amaretto and vanilla until smooth. Add the eggs, one at a time, beating well after each addition. Pour filling over crust, reserving ½ cup (125 mL) of the filling. Mix the reserved filling with the melted chocolate. Drop by spoonfuls onto the filling and swirl into a pattern with a knife.
4. Bake for 10 minutes. Reduce heat to 250°F (120°C) and bake for 30 to 35 minutes or until centre of the cake is barely firm. Remove from oven and run a knife around the sides of the cake. Cool completely before removing sides. Chill until firm. To garnish, soften chocolate squares until a vegetable peeler can be drawn down the short side of each square to form a curl. Mound chocolate curls on cake.

# Index

Produced exclusively for Corning Canada Inc., 60 Leek Crescent, Richmond Hill, Ontario Canada L4B 1H1 by Alpha Corporation/Susan Yates, Publisher
Photographs by Peter Paterson/Paterson Photographic Works Inc.
Copy Editor: Wendy Thomas
Editorial Services: Colborne Communications Centre
Text and Cover Design: Dave Murphy/ArtPlus Ltd.
Page Layout: Valerie Bateman & Leanne Knox/ArtPlus Ltd.
Printed and bound in Canada by Transcontinental Printing Inc.

For product information call: 905-771-3575

ISBN: 1-896391-25-7

Distributed by Canadian Tire Corporation